Module 4
Nontruths Told About
Mary Magdalen

KIM CINTIO

BALBOA.PRESS
A DIVISION OF HAY HOUSE

Balboa Press books may be ordered through booksellers or by contacting:

Balboa Press
A Division of Hay House
1663 Liberty Drive
Bloomington, IN 47403
www.balboapress.com
844-682-1282

Because of the dynamic nature of the Internet, any web addresses or links contained in this book may have changed since publication and may no longer be valid. The views expressed in this work are solely those of the author and do not necessarily reflect the views of the publisher, and the publisher hereby disclaims any responsibility for them.

The author of this book does not dispense medical advice or prescribe the use of any technique as a form of treatment for physical, emotional, or medical problems without the advice of a physician, either directly or indirectly. The intent of the author is only to offer information of a general nature to help you in your quest for emotional and spiritual well-being. In the event you use any of the information in this book for yourself, which is your constitutional right, the author and the publisher assume no responsibility for your actions.

Any people depicted in stock imagery provided by Getty Images are models, and such images are being used for illustrative purposes only.
Certain stock imagery © Getty Images.

Cover Design – Saint Tone Productions.
Painting of Mary Magdalen by Kim Cintio

MaryMuntoldTRUEstory@gmail.com
Indivinetime.com

Print information available on the last page.

ISBN: 978-1-9822-7112-1 (sc)
ISBN: 978-1-9822-7113-8 (e)

Balboa Press rev. date: 10/21/2021

I dedicate this book and these teachings to every beautiful soul who has crossed my path. You have shared your message to me directly and indirectly. In turn, you gave me the drive to move forward on my journey to share the light.

To my mother, Sandra, for all your love and support throughout the years. Thank you for believing in me to make this all possible. My mom passed away prior to the completion of the book. She now watches over me and will see it all from a higher perspective.

I love you, Mom!

❧ Contents ❧

✎ Acknowledgments ✐

I am extremely grateful to have this opportunity to share Mary's untold *true* story of her life *in her own words.* The bond we share is indescribable. Since learning that she shares my physical body, I have felt her every emotion while writing this book and her teachings. For this, I am eternally grateful. It has been my honor to share her untold story.

To my dear brother, Steve, and nephews, Michael and Scott, for your love and support during the process of writing this book.

Janie Boisclair, my special friend. Thank you for your kindness and expertise in helping me to edit and in sharing your knowledge to assist me in the making of this book with Mary's untold story and teachings. I appreciate you!

❧ Introduction ❧

I have been a psychic medium, known as a trance channel medium, a clairvoyant (psychic clear seeing), clairaudient (psychic clear hearing), claircognizance (psychic clear sense of knowing), clairsentient (psychic clear feeling; empathy), and clairalience (psychic clear smelling) most of my life. I am delighted to share with you the direct channeling I received from Mary Magdalen herself in the hopes that it will enlighten you as to the truths about her life that have *not been told to date.*

Mary asks that you read her story with an open heart and mind to allow her words to infiltrate your being and to allow you to immerse in her truth in *her own words.* You will not find any of this material in any other form of written history or literature of any type, including the Bible, gospels, etc.

My spiritual awakening began in 2006. However, this sacred activation brought so much clarity and awareness forward for me to really understand what was coming together for my future endeavors.

In 2016, while on a sacred journey in Sedona, Arizona, I had a miraculous activation take place while I walked the medicine wheel at Amitabha Stupa Peace Park. It was there in the medicine wheel I was spiritually greeted by five sacred elder ancestors of the land. When they approached me, they cleansed me with sage, also known as smudging, as I smelled it. (Burning sage is used to cleanse a person or space of negative energy, unwanted spirits, or stagnated energies. It is an ancient spiritual ritual and a Native American tradition.) They also blessed me speaking in a language that was foreign to me. It sounded like it was in tongues or chanting like. I immediately felt the love and blessing overwhelm me. A sense of greatness was happening. They then asked me to stand in each direction while they continued to cleanse and bless me.

After they finished, I realized that something of great magnitude had just taken place. I went into the middle of the medicine wheel, stood there, looked up at the heavens with my arms outstretched, and expressed my gratitude. It was at that time that one of the women in my group came by and took a picture of me. That night, when I went to sleep, I had a vivid dream. In the dream, I saw myself with my heart wide-open and sharing massive amounts of love to the masses, including all humanity, the animal and plant kingdoms, and the world.

As I sit here writing this, I feel such an immense amount of gratitude for this amazing journey I am on. It was from this moment forward that I realized what was coming forward for me.

Through my channeling experiences, I have learned of my closeness to Mary and how she has already influenced my life.

My hope for you is to find and understand not only the truth about her journey from her own words but also how her wisdom has changed your life.

❧ Chapter 1 ❧

The Sisterhood of the Rose

All italicized print is Mary channeled through Kim Cintio.

Greetings, my beloved children of the light. I would like to share with you at this time about the Sisterhood of the Rose. This name was given to us as the rose symbolizes unconditional love as we, the Magdalens, conveyed. This name also brings forth God and Goddess energy in all forms of the light. It was part of our mission and role of who we were.

There were many of us during that time. Some of the women you may be aware of are Mary Salome, Myriam of Tyana, Mary Anna (Mother Mary), Esther Salome, Elizabeth, and Martha of Bethany (my sister). There will be many more who are listed in the book that I wrote through Kim.

The sisterhood took great pride and pleasure getting together on a daily basis to meditate and practice our connection with the divine. We considered ourselves the highest of highest priestesses of them all. We took great pride in all that we did. This energy even carries over into this present day.

There are many who believe that they are me incarnated. You, my dear children, carry my essence within you and in your DNA. I want you to know that I have not *incarnated since my lifetime with Yeshua. There is a very good chance that you may be one of my sisters from the Sisterhood of the Rose. You see, my dear children, we all had that same drive and persona to make sure we were understood. We often would sit in a circle and share energy or space. Many times, we were inseparable. We would also practice energy healing on each other and share the divine along with the children. We would discuss different types of tantric techniques, often draw pictures, and share how one might be better than another. (Tantra is the Sanskrit word that means "woven together." Hindu and Buddhist use the sexual union as a metaphor for weaving together the physical and the spiritual—weaving humanity to the divine. Sacred sexuality.)*

Note: My Personal Perspective

This channeling was my introduction to the Sisterhood of the Rose. Once I received this information, I reviewed my thoughts and determined I too am a Sister of the Rose. I have such a close relationship with Mary that she has raised my ability to understand and resonate with her as a whole. Through this channeling, I realize that her history is in alignment with my belief system. I also relate to their method of drawing pictures to express their inner soul as I have become a spiritual artist as well. I find myself painting and channeling portraits of spirit guides as well as my personal visions, allowing their energy to infiltrate into the paintings. I feel that by giving myself permission to allow their energy to be present in my life, I have also increased my desire to produce artwork in their honor.

Workbook Questions

❧ Chapter 1 ❧

The Sisterhood of the Rose

1. Do you have a group of likeminded women or men who you can call your sisterhood or brotherhood? Name them.

_____

_____

_____

_____

_____

_____

_____

_____

2. Do you feel you can confide in others and share your secrets?

_____

_____

_____

_____

_____

_____

3. How would you compare your sisterhood or brotherhood to Mary's? Please describe in detail.

_____

_____

_____

_____

_____

_____

If you do not have a group to confide in, use your manifesting skills to bring a sisterhood or brotherhood to you.

Here is one way to manifest:

> *Sit quietly and meditate and see yourself with your ideal group. See, feel, and know that this group has already been formed. Actively sense and see yourself participating with the group. Know in your heart that they are here and waiting for this initiation and connection to take place. See it, feel it, and know it, and it will be. Once you put it out to the Universe, we will activate your desire and create the opportunity to arrive for you to harness for yourself.*

4. Who would you like to manifest into your sisterhood or brotherhood?

_____

_____

_____

_____

_____

_____

❧ Chapter 2 ❧

The Fountain of Love

Greetings, my dear children. I would like to share with you all a sacred place in southern France that is very close to my heart. Upon walking in the woods around the Languedoc area with Yeshua and some of the other Magdalens, we discovered a body of water that had a small waterfall and a heart-shaped pond. It was here that we began to do spiritual cleansings, initiations, baptisms, and sacred baths. We would come here frequently. It gave us great joy to just sit and meditate by the water. It was very serene, secluded, and safe being deep in the woods. Undisturbed, one might say. When we held ceremony here, we felt a strong sense of deep connection to the divine. The water acts as a natural conduit to receive information into the senses.

On many occasions while I was performing an activation, initiation, or baptism, I felt my whole body quiver and go into a trancelike state. During that time, I knew that I had a greater purpose. I never questioned it. I just moved forward with the task that was expected of me. It was quite invigorating, I must add!

I always felt complete after experiencing miraculous healings of this nature. I felt inclined to return and do more. We loved to bring the children there. During these visits, we felt very much at peace, as everyone could be childlike and thoroughly enjoy themselves, both children and adults. It was a blissful way to release all worries and troubles we were experiencing.

Note: My Personal Perspective

I am so grateful and appreciative that I personally had the pleasure of visiting some of Mary's sacred spots in southern France. I had an amazing experience at the fountain of love. While I was looking at the water, hearing and feeling the sounds and the vibrations, I immediately saw myself standing there while receiving a reviving sensation of being lifted into another dimension. It was as if I were receiving a new activation. (Activation is a new energy source that provides additional clarity on a given subject.) I knew that my activation was preparing me for new and exciting opportunities that are now showing themselves and are helping me in the preparation of this workbook through guidance. You will also find this vibration in my book titled *The Untold True Story of Mary Magdalen in Her Own Words.*

Workbook Questions

 Chapter 2

The Fountain of Love

1. Where can you go that is peaceful to meditate and connect to the divine? If you do not have a place to go, just create one.

_____

_____

_____

_____

_____

_____

_____

2. Have you had any experiences similar to what Mary has described while being in a sacred place? Explain and share your details.

_____

_____

_____

_____

_____

_____

3. Have you experienced any type of ceremonial miracles with water? Please share your experiences.

_____

_____

_____

_____

_____

_____

4. In what place of undisturbed nature do you go to receive information from the divine?

_____

_____

_____

_____

_____

_____

_____

∞

Note: Message from Lord Melchizedek

It is of the greatest importance to find a sacred place to call your own to bring forth information from the divine to share all that you have with the ones you feel will benefit with the true wisdom of your soul. This is what Mary, Yeshua, and the Magdalens had: a sacred place they could call their own to be undisturbed and to receive the divine flow of information with the power of the water.

❧ Chapter 3 ❧

Nontruths Told about Mary

My beloved children, I would like to share with you the truth of my life. Not to be confused with any written literature that you may have previously read, such as your Bible and the gospels. The truth will be spoken right here and right now as to what was previously written in these modules and classes taught by me and in the book as channeled through Kim. As previously stated, Yeshua and I were twin flames. Yes, we were lovers and best friends and we were married. We had three biological children (Sar'h or Sarah, Lizbeth, and James) and two adopted children. Yeshua did survive the crucifixion, and he did accompany me to southern Gaul, which is now southern France. I was not a prostitute. That was written out of jealously in a patriarchal society because the church did not want to include a powerful, driven female as part of its religious sect. You see, my children of the light, the Bible was written more than three hundred years after our lifetime in a patriarchal society to take control of the people, so to speak, and to eliminate women as an important part of society.

Now everything is changing as it is time for the New Earth to birth. The divine feminine is coming back into power. In many societies, the matriarch is in charge. In the New Earth, both roles—the divine feminine and the divine masculine—will be equal. Society will be heart centered and practice unconditional love in all aspects of life. The animal, plant, and mineral kingdoms and humanity will all be living in unity with one another. There will be no more lower-vibrating energy circulating. No more fear, hate, greed, or pain on your planet. The end result will be beautiful. We know you will be pleased with it all.

Note: My Personal Perspective

My religious upbringing did not introduce me to Mary. I had to learn from other publications and my own experiences while traveling to Europe and the United Kingdom and walking in her footsteps. I am extremely grateful that on my trip to France, Mary chose to come through and educate me about her true-life journey. I realized that there were very few publications that had the *true* story. This is why it is important for me to share what I have learned. I believe I will continue to share this information through the balance of my life in Mary's honor.

Workbook Questions

 Chapter 3

Nontruths Told about Mary

1. Now that you have learned the truth about Mary and Yeshua's lifetime, how do you feel?

_____

_____

_____

_____

_____

_____

_____

_____

_____

2. Does it make you change your opinions and values of what you have learned in your own life?

_____

_____

_____

_____

_____

_____

3. Are you able to read it with an open heart, putting aside all the untruths that have been written and contorted throughout the years?

_____

_____

_____

_____

_____

_____

4. Can you resonate with how Mary felt while trying to be heard in a patriarchal society?

(She pushed through the resistance to follow her mission.)

_____

_____

_____

_____

_____

_____

_____

 confused

Congratulations!

You have just completed module 4. To learn about Mary's untold *true* story and teachings, see the other modules that are available.

Module 1 - My Introduction to Mary Magdalen and How She Came into My Awareness
Module 2 - Mary Magdalen's Current Sacred Mission
Module 3 - Mary Magdalen's Relationship with Archangel Michael

Learn more, shared in detail, in the book titled *The Untold True Story of Mary Magdalen in Her Own Words.*

Printed in the United States
by Baker & Taylor Publisher Services